MARRIAGE OF HONOR

A Premarital Counseling Course
Participant's Notebook

J. Morris Beene

ISBN 979-8-88644-313-4 (Paperback)
ISBN 979-8-88644-314-1 (Digital)

Covenant Books
11661 Hwy 707
Murrells Inlet, SC 29576
www.covenantbooks.com

First, I would like to dedicate this book to my wife, Kendra. Due to her loving support through years of counseling ministry, I have learned and seen how these principles of *Marriage of Honor* hold true.

Second, I would like to thank you for purchasing this book. It is my prayer that you will be able to use it in your premarital counseling setting to help couples further develop a sense of what marriage is intended to be—to represent the relationship of Jesus Christ and the church, His bride. May God richly bless your marriage.

Now to him who is able to do far more abundantly than all that we ask or think, according to the power at work within us, to him be glory in the church and in Christ Jesus throughout all generations, forever and ever. Amen.

Ephesians 3:20-21

Lesson 1
Marriage: A Covenant with God

*No marriage ever stays the same—it
either gets better, or it gets worse.*

1. *God ordained marriage*
   A. Marriage is not optional in God's design—to be
   married or be single and celibate.

   B. God Himself created and ordained marriage.

   C. Marriage is a covenantal relationship: *the covenant of companionship* (Proverbs 2:17; Malachi 2:14).
      1. From God

      2. The elements of an Old Testament covenant (Genesis 15:1–21)

      3. Each of the elements of the Old Testament covenant is carried into the typical modern-day wedding ceremony.

D. Marriage is good.
   1. Significant difference between the companionship of marriage and celibacy.

   2. God says of marriage…

   3. Celibacy is not higher (1 Corinthians 7:1–7).

2. *God ordained marriage for His purposes*
   A. To represent (Ephesians 5:21–33)

   B. Meet a basic need:

   C. This companionship provides for (Genesis 2:18):
      1.

      2.

      3.

3. God ordained marriage to provide for separate decision-making units (Genesis 2:24). This is called the family.

A. God calls for a leaving

B. God calls for a cleaving

C. Parents *must*

D. Children *must*

4. *Since God ordained the marriage, He intended for there to be a permanent relationship found in marriage and there is a temporary relationship.*

A. Permanent

B. Temporary

C. Because of this permanent/temporary relationship, difference exists…

Homework: Renewing Your Covenant with God (Work on this assignment as soon as you can.)

Renew Your Covenant with God

1. There is a need to make a covenant with God. What in your life is God leading you to rededicate to Him? "Now I intend to make a covenant with the Lord" (2 Chronicles 29:10).

2. The church should prepare for the coming of the Lord. The Lord's bride has prostituted herself with worldly priorities and methods. (Ephesians 5:25–26)

3. Many leaders remain in personal sin and disobedience (Jeremiah 23). The need is to confess and forsake sin and to lead the people to corporate repentance (1 John 1:9; 2 Chronicles 7:14).

4. Questions (answer each prayerfully and honestly):
   a. Do I foster the bitter antagonisms of days gone by (Luke 11:47–51)?
   b. Do I keep the letter of the law and not the Spirit (Luke 11:42)?
   c. Do I try to disguise my spiritual deadness (Luke 11:44)?
   d. Do I need revival? What specifically do I want to see happen this week?

Ask God to do extraordinary things (Joel 2:14).

Awakening in the New Testament is Christ-centered. It involves a deep sense of genuine humility before God.

5. Prayer for revival
    ➤ How do I repent? Search your heart (Psalm 139:23–24).
    ➤ Make every effort to keep the unity of the Spirit through the bond of peace. There is one body and one Spirit (Ephesians 4:3–4).
    ➤ Has it been a long time since there was a fresh testimony of God's grace in a personal experience?
    ➤ Do you sense that God has withdrawn His presence from you (Micah 3:4)?
    ➤ All confessions should be under the direction of the Holy Spirit. Ask the Holy Spirit to reveal to you any sin that you are guilty of knowingly or unknowingly.
    ➤ God is ready to pour out His Spirit on His people and bring great numbers of lost people to salvation after we repent (Joel 2:28–32)
    ➤ Expect God to give you great victories (2 Chronicles 32:1–23).
    ➤ Verse 22: "The Lord took care of them on every side."

Study this information on covenantal relationships with God. As a believer, you entered a covenantal relationship with God. If you are married, you entered a covenantal relationship with God. If you are an ordained minister or deacon, you entered a covenantal relationship with God. Pray about each covenantal relationship with which you have entered with God, and ask for the assurance that each is right with the Lord.

Lesson 2
Shepherds: A Call from God for the Family

John 10:1–15, "Jesus is the Shepherd of His flock of sheep."

In this passage, Jesus identifies five different "players" in this scenario:
1.

2.

3.

4.

5.

What position does the shepherd take in going out of the sheepfold in Psalm 23:1–6?
First of all, the shepherd ___________________.
He makes the sheep ___________________________.
He leads them ___________________________.
The shepherd ___________________________.
He leads the sheep on ___________________________.
not "___________________."

Who is the enemy?

What is the "hired hand"?

The shepherd is the _________________ of the sheepfold.

There is a "microshepherd" of the "microflock."

WHO is the "microshepherd"?

WHO is the "microflock"?

WHO poses the greatest risk and danger to your wife (Ephesians 5:23)?

You have the choice today and every day to either

1.

Or

2.

Be her "microshepherd."

Also as "microshepherd," you _________________________.

"Too many families have been _________________________."

Family Job Description in Walking with the Lord (Psalm 96:1–13)

There are ten verbs in this passage that describe our interaction with God…

1.

2.

3.

4.

5.

6.

7.

8.

9.

10.

Romans 8:19
Families need _______________________________
No such thing as _______________________________

Lesson 3
Love Languages

Each one of us has the capacity to express love in many different ways. There are five types of love languages. During the dating phase of our relationships, most people will speak love in all five love languages, trying to truly get the point across to our intended "target" for love. Each of us feels loved when someone else speaks love to us in any of the five love languages. However, each person has a primary love language. *And* each person has a different or unique pattern of love languages.

Five Love Languages

1. Words
2. Gift giving
3. Acts of service
4. Quality time
5. Physical touch and closeness

Homework Assignment

Find your mate's primary love language by doing the following exercise: List below in the first column *your* primary love language, the way you feel the most loved, and the other four in descending order of importance. Then, list your mate's primary love language and his/her other four in descending order. Then compare your findings.

Yours:
  Primary: _________
      2: _________
      3: _________
      4: _________
      5: _________

Your mate's:
  Primary_________
      2: _________
      3: _________
      4: _________
      5: _________

Allow the discussion to lead to *learning—not argument*. When your mate identifies his/her primary, *believe* them—do not say, "That is not your primary…" Use this as a valuable learning experience about your mate's love needs.

Lesson 4
God's Plan for Responsibilities in Marriage

Ephesians 5:21–31
I. *Submission is a commandment.*
II. *Wife, be submissive to your husband.*
  A. Does this mean,

  B. Does this mean,

  C. Does this mean,

  D. This means:

III. *Who is the head of the household* (Proverbs 31:10ff)?
IV. *The husband is the head of the wife.*
  1   This means:

  2   Please note this is NOT

  3   The husband is to love the wife

V. *The wife is to treat her husband with respect—NOT nagging or being contentious* (Proverbs 21:9, 19; 1 Peter 3:1–6).

VI. *The role of the husband: the submissive leader*

   1   Responsibility (Ephesians 5:25)

   2   Submission (Ephesians 5:21)

   3   Spiritual head

   4   Die to self for the wife

   5   Upholding the wife (1 Peter 3:7)

God's best is…

Lesson 5
Communication in the Marriage

Communication between two or more individuals is a fine art, which must be refined, and the skills must be reviewed continuously to keep them honed to a sharp edge.

Communication is like a radio wave: there must be a transmitter and a receiver, both on the same frequency so that effective communication can take place. That means, the sender and the receiver must be on the same wavelength so that clear, concise, understandable communication is the result. That should be the key for all your communications: to express your ideas clearly and in an understandable manner so that the receiver will know exactly what you are trying to say.

Listening
One key to communication is listening. Listening is an ______!

There are at least five things that must be considered every time you try to communicate with your mate…

1.

2.

3.

4.

5.

Using feedback…
Work on the following homework assignments when you return home after this weekend.

Homework
Conference Table Instructions

One practical method for helping achieve unity in communication within a couple is to use a *conference table*. This should be a literal table in the home that is not used often for other things. Some couples use a game table set up every evening for this specific purpose. The use of the conference table will help you establish the habit of solving problems daily rather than letting them stack up over several days or several weeks, building frustration, anger, bitterness, etc. The daily use of the conference table will allow you to solve the day's problems before they become bigger than they need to be.

Place

Agree upon an area in which daily conferences may be held without interruptions. Choose a table, preferably one that is not used frequently for other purposes. Hold all conferences there. If problems arise elsewhere, whenever possible wait until you reach home to discuss them—at the conference table, of course. The first week read Ephesians 4:17–32 each night before conferring.

Place: _______________________________

Time: _______________________________

Purpose

The conference table is a place to confer, not to argue. Begin by talking about yourself—your sins and failures—and settle all such matters first by asking forgiveness (Matthew 7:4–5). Speak the truth in love, gently. Do not allow any concern to be carried over into the next day. Not all problems can be solved in one sitting. You may find it necessary to make up an agenda and schedule out the work over a period of time according to priorities. Direct all your energies toward defeating the problem, not toward the other person. Your goal is to reach biblical solutions, so always have Bibles on the table and use them. It helps to record the results of your work on paper. Open and close all conferences with prayer. When you need help, reread Ephesians 4:25–32.

Procedures

If any conferee clams up or does anything other than confer at the table, the other must rise and stand quietly. This prearranged signal means "In my opinion, we've stopped conferring." Whether he/she was right or wrong in this judgment does not matter and ought not to be discussed at the moment. The person seated should then indicate his/her willingness to confer and invite the other to be seated again.

Lists may be brought to the conference table, but remember, this time is to confer about differences and needed solutions, not a place to fix blame or to argue about the other person's perceptions.

Remember: Perception is reality until perception is changed.

Homework
Communication Guidelines

1. Be a ready listener, and do not answer until the other person has finished talking (Proverbs 19;13; James 1:19).
2. Be slow to speak (Proverbs 15:23, 28; 29:20; James 1:19).
3. Do not go to bed angry (Ephesians 4:15, 25; Colossians 3:8; Matthew 6:34)!
4. Do not use silence to frustrate the other person (Proverbs 10:19; 15:28; 16:21, 23; 18:2; 20:15; Colossians 4:6).
5. Do not become involved in quarrels (Proverbs 17:14; 20:3; Romans 13:13; Ephesians 4:31).
6. Do not respond in uncontrolled anger (Proverbs 14:29; 15:1; 25:15; 29:11; Ephesians 4:26, 31).
7. When you are in the wrong, admit it and ask for forgiveness (Proverbs 12:15; 16:2; 20:6; 21:2; Matthew 5:23–25; Luke 17:3; James 5:16).
8. When someone confesses to you, offer forgiveness without hesitation (Proverbs 17:9; Ephesians 4:32; Colossians 3:13; 1 Peter 4:8).
9. Avoid nagging (Proverbs 10:19; 16:21, 23; 17:9; 18:6, 7; 21:19; 27:15).
10. Do not blame or criticize the other person (Romans 14:13; Galatians 6:1; 1 Thessalonians 5:11).
11. If someone verbally attacks, criticizes, or blames you, do not respond in the same manner (Romans 12:17, 21; 1 Peter 2:23; 3:9).

12. Try to understand the other person's opinions.
13. Be concerned about the other person's interests (Ephesians 4:2; Philippians 2:4; 3:15, 16).

What you have just studied are biblical directives for promoting good communication and good relationships with other people. To really put some teeth into your effort to become more biblical in your communication, you may wish to sign the following agreement to implement these guidelines (husband and wife both sign).

Name _______________________________________

Date _______________________________________

Name _______________________________________

Date _______________________________________

Lesson 6
God's Blueprint for Forgiveness

There are at least five misconceptions about forgiveness:

1.

2.

3.

4.

5.

First of all, *what is forgiveness?*
Forgiveness is _______________________ (Psalm 103:12).

To debunk the five misconceptions, let's consider these truths.

    1. Forgive and forget…

Not remembering…

Forgetting…

1 Corinthians 13:4–8

2. Apologizing?

3. Forgiveness is not a feeling.

Matthew 18:21–22

Matthew 6:14, 15

4. Forgiving yourself?

1 John 1:9

5. Forgiveness is conditional.

1 Peter 4:8

Proverbs 17:9

Repentance precedes forgiveness from God—every time.
Colossians 3:12–13

Luke 17:3–4

Two points that bear repeating:
1. God does not…

2. God does not…

Remember the saying of my brother, Harold Jones:

If you do things the Bible way, you get Bible results!

Additional Notes on Confession:
(Copied by Permission from Peace Makers)

There are seven elements to a good confession:
1. Address every person involved in the offense, including God (Psalm 32:5).

2. Avoid "if," "but," and/or "maybe" in the confession. Make the confession real.

3. Admit specifically the offense—do not speak in generalities.

4. Acknowledge the hurt in the other person that you caused.

5. Accept the consequences.

6. Alter your behavior.

7. Ask forgiveness (those words specifically, not "I'm sorry" or "I apologize"), and allow the other person time to work through the hurt and consequences with you (1 John 1:9).

Four promises of forgiveness:
1. I will not dwell on this incident.

2. I will not bring this incident up and use it against you.

3. I will not talk to others about this incident.

4. I will not allow this incident to stand between us or hinder our personal relationship.

Homework

1. When you go back home or to your room this evening, work specifically through the Sin List assignment. This may take as long as two to three hours, but it is vital to work through it as part of this renewal weekend. Even if you have done something similar in the past, work through this at this time as well—you may have a short Sin List, but there may be things that God will reveal to you this time that has not come up before.

2. After working through your Sin List, if there are any issues that you need to address with your mate, then prayerfully and carefully speak with your mate about those issues, seeking forgiveness from one another *and* offering forgiveness to one another, following the principles covered during the evening session on forgiveness. Keep in mind that there may be things that need to be addressed *only* with God—but if there are those things that have impacted your marriage, then you need to speak with your mate about those items. [*Note*: Make the confession as public as the knowledge of the sin. If it is between you and God, keep it there… Don't share.]

3. Now, ask your mate if there are any major (potentially relationship-breaking) offenses you have not addressed that need to be forgiven—your mate may be aware of things you have done that have caused

a major offense. Therefore, these need to be worked through as well.

Note: Every session of confrontation/forgiveness *must* end with a reaffirmation of your love toward one another. Do not ever skip this part of the healing process.

Sin List Homework Assignment

This assignment will help lead you to a deeper relationship with God through Jesus Christ. When we need to draw closer to God, we need to be cleaner from our own transgressions (sins) as part of that experience. God says to "wash your hands" (James 4:8). This is a word picture of the high priest in the Old Testament stopping at the laver (bronze basin) to wash the blood from his hands (following the sacrifice for the redemption of the sins of the people) before he would approach the Holy of Holies to be drawn into the presence of Jehovah God. We also need that cleansing work that takes place by the washing of the Word of God in our lives and the cleansing of the Holy Spirit. There are several steps to work through in this cleansing and may take several hours of prayer to work through this process. Plan to spend at least two hours with God in prayer in this time of cleansing. You will need your Bible and a tablet and pencil or pen to write some things down.

1. Read Psalm 139:23–24

> Search me O God, and know my heart; Try me and know my anxious thoughts; And see if there be any hurtful way in me, and lead me in the everlasting way.

2. Now, read 1 John 1:9—our *"spiritual bar of soap"*

> If we confess our sins, He is faithful
> and righteous to forgive us our sins and
> to cleanse us of all unrighteousness.

3. Third, now pray these two verses to God asking Him to search you, try you, and show you things in your life that you either (1) need forgiveness for or (2) need cleansing. You see, many times, we accept that forgiveness from God but forget to get clean. Keep in mind the truth in *Romans 8:1,* "There is therefore now no condemnation for those who are in Christ Jesus." God wants to cleanse you and does not condemn you for these sins—He simply wants you to be closer to Him.

4. As God reveals things to you, write them down on your Sin List. Don't question the things that come to mind—even if they happened many years ago, write them down—even if you have already been forgiven, write them down because you may simply need to seek that cleansing from God.

5. After you have the list as complete as you think it can be (God may well indicate that you are finished with that by not bringing anything else to mind), then begin with item 1 on your list and (1) confess the sin (agree with God that it was sin and that you did that particular sin), (2) thank Him for the forgiveness provided by Jesus Christ, and (3) ask Him to cleanse you of the sin. Stay on each item until you feel clean.

Work through these one at a time, being honest with yourself before God—and you will come away from this experience with a renewed sense of being clean before God.

Two warnings:

1. There may be some items on the list that require restitution (repaying something or someone). If so, make a commitment to God to take care of those items one at a time as you are able to do so. Be sure you keep this commitment.

2. Keep the confession as private as the knowledge of the sin. There may be some things that may require going to another person and asking for their forgiveness. However, keep in mind that if they are not aware of the situation (for example, a thought-life problem that no one else is aware of), you need to keep it between you and God. It does not need to go any further than that and may actually harm relationships rather than help them.

If you have any questions, please be sure and ask as you work through this assignment.

Lesson 7
Parenting God's Way

Children Are Special

Please, Mom And Dad...
My hands are small—I don't mean to spill my milk.
My legs are short—Please slow down
so I can keep up with you.
Don't slap my hands when I touch something
bright and pretty—I don't understand.
Please look at me when I talk to you—It
lets me know you are really listening.
My feelings are tender—Don't nag me all day.
Let me make mistakes without feeling stupid.
Don't expect the bed I make or the picture I
draw to be perfect—Just Love Me for Trying.
Remember I am a child, not a small adult—
sometimes I don't understand what you are saying.
I Love You So Much—Please Love Me just for
being Me—Not just for the things I do.

—Author anonymous

I. *Introduction*
   First of all, we must realize that we are not under
   Old Testament Law.
   Deuteronomy 21:18–21

So, how are we as Christian parents supposed to deal with our children in today's society?

Ephesians 6:4

Colossians 3:21

II. *Basics of parenting*
   A. Listening to your children
   B. Fathers, do not provoke your children to anger (Ephesians 6:4)
      1. Expecting

      2. Giving instructions

      3. Putting them in

      4. Holding them

Rather:
      1. Uphold them

2. Praise them

3. Teaching by

4. Live a life

C. Focus your attention on your child.
D. Teach obedience
   1. *Immediate*

There are three "problem patterns" in parenting:
   a.

   b.

   c.

2. *Complete*

3. *Cheerful*

E. Teaching ethics
Proverbs 20:11

III. *Discipline vs. chastisement*
Proverbs 29:15

Proverbs 29:17

Proverbs 13:24

Proverbs 29:15

IV. *How to love your children*
A. Love their mother

B. Love their father

C. Love the child

V. *How to love your teen*
A. Make the home.

B. Make the family.

C. Listen to them.

D. Communicate with them.

E. Make contact.

F. Build an understanding.

G. Choose wisely.

Lesson 8
God's Creation of Men and Women:
Celebrate the Differences

Introduction
The Differences

The key difference
    Men are

    Women are

Let's consider a few general, everyday tasks and look at the different characteristic approaches made by the majority of men and women (not an all-inclusive distinction, by any means).

Shopping
    Men:

    Women:

Traveling
    Men:

Women:

Problem Solving
Men:

Women:

Security in the Relationship
Men:

Women:

Responsibility in the Relationship with God
There is a very real difference that is pointed out in the Bible about the differences in the responsibility in our relationship with God in our marriage.
1. God created Adam first, then Eve (1 Corinthians 11:8, 9)

2. God declared that Adam's existence without Eve was not good.

3. After they both sinned,

4. When God confronted the hiding pair (1 Corinthians 15:22, 45),

5. God's judgment on Eve was

So what is the true nature of masculinity and femininity? Two truths emerge as you study the Bible about the man and woman in marriage:
1. Every husband has

2. Every wife has

Bottom line: We are *not* called to be self-centered, but we *are* called to be other-oriented by God. Only when we are truly other-oriented will God openly bless our relationships as husband and wife.

Lesson 9
Ethics in Marriage

Introduction
Principles of Conduct in Marriage

Do's
  1.

  2.

  3.

  4.

  5.

  6.

  7.

  8.

9.

10.

Don'ts
1.

2.

3.

4.

5.

6.

7.

8.

Lesson 10
Expressing Intimacy (Physical Relationship)

Final Session of Premarital Counseling
The Physical Relationship

[*Note*: This document on the physical relationship is characteristically given to the couple the week prior to their wedding (can be emailed or mailed).]

Now, since we are just *one* week away from the wedding, we can cover the last session in print rather than in person. (With little to no embarrassment this way!) Actually, there is nothing to be embarrassed about—this is a gift from God.

I also wanted to address a couple of issues of what the physical relationship is intended to be in marriage and what it is *not* intended to be.

First and foremost, the physical relationship is intended to be a blessing from God—not something to create the relationship, not something to fix a broken relationship, not something to be used as a bargaining chip, and not something to be used to frustrate or hurt one another. It is intended truly as a physical union between the husband and wife, and when the attitudes of the couple are right, it is truly a worshipful experience. Prior to marriage, sex is simply a sinful act of fornication. Inside marriage, God intended it as an expression of unity and closeness that cannot be achieved any other way. For in the very act of sexual intercourse, there is no other way to be any closer physically than in that act of love—this act truly fulfills the statement of Genesis 2:24—being "one flesh" speaks of this unity and closeness.

I said earlier that this would not be a how-to session but one addressing attitudes and specifics of what God called this act to be. And so, I want you to read 1 Corinthians 7:1–5. In this passage, Paul describes the basics of the physical relationship in attitude. First of all, Paul says in verse 2 that each man should have his own wife *only*, and each woman should have her own husband (*only*). This speaks of an absolutely exclusive relationship between the husband and wife—not to be shared with anyone else or given to anyone else—not to be talked about with anyone else and not to have anyone else participate. The marriage bed is to remain absolutely holy—undefiled and exclusive. The next verse refers to the duty of the husband and wife—what is that duty? Remember the passage in Ephesians 5:21—being submissive? This means again to "meet the other one's needs." This is a vital concept as we progress through this session. The goal is to meet the other one's needs at all times, not focusing on your own needs but on the needs of the other. The duty then is to meet the other person's needs as much as you can.

When out of balance, one person can use this concept to manipulate the situation, as in, "You have to meet my needs! My needs are for sex…" The way it should be is, "What are your needs?" Find out and then meet the other's needs. Asking the other rather than demanding *of* the other is the key to making this work as God intended it to be.

In 1 Corinthians 7:4—this verse talks about authority. This *does not* mean that the husband has the authority to do whatever he wants to do to the wife, nor that the wife has the authority to do whatever she wants to the husband. What this *does* mean is that the husband has the authority to *meet the wife's needs* and the wife should *meet the husband's needs*. The authority of each has dealt with fulfilling the other, not using the other's body to fulfill their own selfish desires. I hope this is a clear explanation. For example, the husband wants to make love—the wife does not. So what happens? The husband, as the leader and typically initiator, recognizes this is not a good time and meets her needs by *not* initiating sexual relations. Now it could also work the opposite, and as the wife recognizes the husband's needs, she makes a deterministic decision to fulfill those for him. In doing so, both the husband and the wife are "giving" to the other, and it is a sweet reminder of what God called for in marriage. When approached like this, there is never any demanding but only gentle love. Got the picture? It is not about physical performance, not about physical attributes—but it is about attitude and affection for the other.

Verse 5 gives an instruction about being careful to not deprive one another of this blessing of physical love for extended periods—this leads to temptation that neither the husband nor wife needs—except for a season of prayer.

So keep each other's needs in mind—meet those needs, and then God intends the husband and the wife to enjoy the experience. For specifics, I would recommend the book by Dr. Ed Wheat entitled *Intended for Pleasure* that deals with the how-to aspect of the physical relationship. He provides some wonderful insights into this relationship.

I will add a couple of things though. First, *always be tender with one another*. Husband, always use a gentle, soft touch with the wife—and remember, there is one concept most husbands have to learn: if she says she does not like a certain kind of touch—more of that same touch will not help her like it anymore. If she says "Don't," then *don't*. Be honest and open with each other in communicating what each of you likes. In the practice of touch—even take the other person's hand and show them what you like. This is a very sensual and enjoyable part of the relationship. Experimentation is to be fun— and never painful. Just be honest and open in the communication of what is enjoyable and what is not. And if your partner says, "I don't like that," don't take it as a rejection. Simply ask what to do next…

Second, there are several questions that come up often in counseling in this area that I want to cover at this time:

1. As I said earlier, men tend to be the initiators of most things in the marriage; and the wife, the responder. This tendency is present in communication as well as physical intimacy. Men tend to get frustrated and want the wife to initiate at times, but that is typically not going to be the case. Accept the role that you feel

most comfortable with and enjoy. If the husband needs to initiate, then he should initiate. If the wife tends to be the responder, then she should not work too hard to change that. Keep in mind, at times, the roles may be reversed. Again, don't make demands.

2. There tends to be almost an obsession of the husband with a particular part of the female anatomy. Some wives get very frustrated with the husband's attention to their breasts. There is a reason. God said in Proverbs 5:19 that the breasts of the wife are to satisfy the husband. There is a double meaning here too—*only* the wife's breasts should satisfy the husband, and *don't* get involved in looking, desiring, lusting after any others. In fact, God's Word says that the woman's breasts are created for two things—to feed babies and to satisfy the husband. So if you notice that near obsession, this is why. And it is *natural. But* keep in mind what I said earlier—meet each *other's* needs—so, guys, if there is a need for her to *not* be touched, then don't. This keeps things in balance.

There is no "normal" activity level…if you know what I mean. What works for both of you is then okay. There are some couples I have counseled that have physical relations once per week (this number typically develops after being married for several years, and the "more normal" pattern emerges), and some couples have reported making love as much as twice per day during the week. Obviously, the frequency varies with the couple. There is a tendency for the woman to be more "receptive" during certain times of her menstrual cycle and "less receptive" at other times. You will learn these patterns, and again, these are normal adjustments to marriage and the physical relationship.

As you focus on meeting each other's needs, focusing on continuing to put God in the center of your marriage relationship, and prayerfully spending time with one another, God will bless your relationship richly.

May you experience the full blessings of God in your marriage.

J. Morris Beene
Licensed Professional Counselor

Please remember to practice this little assignment consistently in your marriage.

The Three Ds

Dialogue   Daily Date   Weekly Disappear Occasionally

Complete the following homework assignment after you get home and have more time to pray through this assignment.

Homework Assignment
Nine Ways to Edify Your Mate

1. Make the irrevocable decision to never again be critical of your partner in word, thought, or deed. This may sound like an impossibility, but it is not. It is simply a decision backed up by action until it becomes a habit you would not change if you could.
2. Study your partner. Become sensitive to the areas where your partner feels a lack, and think of ways to build up your partner in those areas particularly.
3. Think every day of positive qualities and behavior patterns you admire, and appreciate in your mate.
4. Consistently verbalize praise and appreciation for your partner. Be genuine, be specific, be generous. You edify with the spoken word.
5. Recognize your partner's talents, abilities, and accomplishments. Communicate your respect for the work he or she does.

6. Husband, show your wife publicly and privately how precious she is to you. And do not express admiration for another woman. This is never edifying to your wife. Keep your attention focused on her!

7. Wife, show your husband that he is the most important person in your life—always. Seek his opinions, and value his judgment.

8. Respond to each other physically and facially. The face is the most distinctive and expressive part of a person. Your mate wants to see you smile, eyes sparkling in response to him or her.

9. Always exhibit the greatest courtesy to each other. You should be VIPs in your own home!

Take time to read this together, and sign each other's page as a sign of your commitment to one another:

_______________________   _______________________
            Name   Name

Copied with permission from *Love Life for Every Married Couple*
by Dr. Ed Wheat

Homework Assignment on Intimacy

Part 1

How satisfied are you with the way you and your mate handle the following aspects of your sexual relationship? Circle the number that corresponds to your answer. Draw an X through each answer that you think your mate will select.

Satisfaction
Low high

1 2 3 4 5 Viewing sex with positive anticipation.

1 2 3 4 5 The way you decide to have sex together.

1 2 3 4 5 The amount of communication during love-making (i.e., discussing better ways of pleasing each other).

1 2 3 4 5 The frequency of your physical intimacy.

1 2 3 4 5 Gentleness and tenderness during lovemaking.

1 2 3 4 5 The variety of your sexual experiences together.

1 2 3 4 5 The understanding I have of my mate in this area.

Part 2

Answer the following questions; use the back of this page if necessary:

1. List any fears you may have about sex. How can your mate alleviate these fears?

2. Do you fully trust your mate with your body? If not, in what aspect? Why?
3. List any incorrect attitudes you may have about your body or your mate's body.

Part 3

Complete the following:

1. When we are sharing physical love, I like for you to…
2. It makes me feel discouraged when you…

Part 4

Look back over parts one through three, and note what changes in your own behavior could make improvements.

1. In prayer, confess any resentment and bitterness you may have.
2. Recognize that sex is a gift from God and that an attitude of giving establishes oneness.
3. List at least one action that you will undertake to improve the physical relationship in your marriage.

Homework Assignment
Twenty-Five Suggestions for Touching

1. When dating, young people can scarcely be kept apart. Most married couples have forgotten how much fun physical closeness can be! So set aside practice times at night (at least once a week) to learn the delights of nonsexual body caressing. Make a date ahead of time. Anticipate pleasure and relaxation together.
2. Show each other where you like to be touched and the kind of touch that pleases you. Usually, a light touch is the most thrilling. Be imaginative in the way you caress.
3. Remember the purpose: to establish a good emotional climate of warmth, love, and affection; *not* to initiate sex. If sex results later because you both want it, that's all right. But you need to learn to enjoy nonsexual touching during these exercise times.
4. Demonstrate to each other how you prefer to be held. Kiss your partner the way you would like to be kissed—not to criticize past performances but to communicate something your partner has not sensed before.
5. Use lotion or baby oil in body caressing; use K-Y Jelly when touching the more sensitive areas of the body. Physical caressing should be totally pleasant.
6. Try caressing (not tickling!) each other's feet. For almost everyone, this is a pleasurable and nonthreatening form of touch communication. Some peo-

ple bathe, dry, and oil each other's feet gently and leisurely.

7. Cleanliness is essential for the enjoyment of these sessions.

8. Some evenings take your shower or bath together. Make this a lighthearted, sensuous experience.

9. Americans habitually do everything in a rush, including lovemaking. But to learn the art of expressing warm sensual feelings, you will have to slow down. If what you are doing feels good, take the time to enjoy it. This may become the best part of your day.

10. Caress each other's back. Pay special attention to the back of the neck at the hairline and the area just above the small of the back.

11. Maintain a positive attitude (the attitude of yes, rather than no). If some manner of caressing or the area chosen does not feel particularly enjoyable, gently lead your partner on to something you do like. Never say "Stop doing that!" or similar words. The atmosphere should be delightfully permissive.

12. Practice communicating warmth. Learn to be emotionally aware of your own feelings and those of your partner. Focus on expressing your love through the medium of touch. Caress each other's faces in the dark, becoming more aware of your partner and spelling out love.

13. Make sure that both of you are having equal opportunities to give and to receive. Take turns giving pleasure to each other.

14. When you caress, use a slow, tender, appreciative touch, indicating how much you enjoy your partner's body—each part of it. When people feel negative about some part of their body, it is more difficult for them to relate freely to their partner. Help your mate realize that every part of his or her body is pleasing, attractive, and desirable to you.

15. Develop positive feelings toward your own body given to you by God. This is biblical! Meditate on Psalm 139:14. "I praise you because I am fearfully and wonderfully made; your works are wonderful, I know that full well."

16. Communicate verbally during your exercises, telling each other what you especially enjoy and how it makes you feel.

17. Sleep in as few clothes as possible at night. Clothes are only a hindrance during these touching sessions.

18. Practice breathing together in rhythm, both of you lying on your side, the other pressed up against your back, hand on your abdomen to gauge your breathing, and adjust his/her rhythm to yours. Then reverse places and do it again.

19. Try to go to bed when your partner does every night.

20. Have a period of fifteen to thirty minutes every night to lie in each other's arms in the dark before you drift off to sleep. Whisper together, sharing private thoughts and pleasant little experiences of the day. Avoid controversial or negative topics. This is the time to build intimacy and wind down for sleep. You will become used to sharing things with each other

that you would not otherwise mention. In each other's arms, the hurts and frustrations of the day are healed. You may want to pray together at this time or just relax in the comfort of physically felt love.

21. Establish the cozy habit of staying in some sort of physical contact while you are going to sleep—a hand or a leg touching your partner's, for instance.

22. Begin every day with a few minutes of cuddling and snuggling before you get out of bed. A husband can tell his wife how nice she feels and how glad he is to be close to her. A wife can nestle in her husband's arms and tell him she wishes they didn't have to leave each other that morning. Just be close and savor gentle physical contact for a while. It will make the morning bout with the alarm clock far more pleasant, so allow a few minutes in your schedule for this even though one or both of you must soon be up and off to work.

23. Hold hands often. Think of all the different ways you can enjoy just touching with your hands and all the different feelings that can be conveyed.

24. Become aware of the many ways you can have physical contact in the course of a week. Touch when you are talking, and maintain eye contact. Sit close to each other in church. Kiss each other when there is no occasion for it. Add variety to your kisses, your touches, and your love pats.

25. While you watch television, make sure you sit close together and use the time for some physical communication. A wise wife will cuddle close to her hus-

band when he chooses to watch his football games even if she is not interested in the program. Since so many people spend so much time before the TV set, it need not be wasted if they are at least together physically.

Copied with permission from *Love Life for Every Married Couple*
by Dr. Ed Wheat

About the Author

J. Morris Beene has been in the counseling ministry in Greenville, Texas, since 1985. He has been in private practice as a biblical counselor in Greenville where he continues to work with people through God's Word to help those in need. During his counseling ministry, Morris has developed a premarital counseling course that he has used since the late 1980s, helping couples who are seeking biblical direction for their upcoming marriage.

Morris and his wife Kendra have been married since August 5, 1978, and have two sons, both married, and they have seven grandchildren. He and Kendra have attended Crosspoint Fellowship since October 2005. He is currently one of the elders at Crosspoint Fellowship and enjoys teaching and preaching when the opportunity arises.

www.ingramcontent.com/pod-product-compliance
Lightning Source LLC
Chambersburg PA
CBHW052240150726
48002CB00003B/1508